Epics for Students, Second Edition, Volume 1

Project Editor: Sara Constantakis Rights Acquisition and Management: Margaret Chamberlain-Gaston, Savannah Gignac, Tracie Richardson, Jhanay Williams Composition: Evi Abou-El-Seoud

Manufacturing: Drew Kalasky

Imaging: John Watkins

Product Design: Pamela A. E. Galbreath, Jennifer Wahi Content Conversion: Katrina Coach Product Manager: Meggin Condino

ISBN-13: 978-1-4144-7621-6 (set)
ISBN-13: 978-1-4144-7622-3 (vol. 1)
ISBN-13: 978-1-4144-7623-0 (vol. 2) ISBN-10: 1-4144-7621-3 (set)
ISBN-10: 1-4144-7622-1 (vol. 1)
ISBN-10: 1-4144-7623-X (vol. 2) This title is also available as an e-book.
ISBN-13: 978-1-4144-7624-7
ISBN-10: 1-4144-7624-8
Contact your Gale, a part of Cengage Learning sales representative for ordering information.

Epic of Gilgamesh

Anonymous

2000 BC

Introduction

Although more than four thousand years old and written originally on tablets of clay, the *Epic of Gilgamesh* continues to fascinate contemporary readers with its account of Gilgamesh, ruler of Uruk; his companion, the "wild man" Enkidu; and their exploits together. Generally recognized as the earliest epic cycle yet known-prior to even the *Iliad* or the *Odyssey*—the *Epic of Gilgamesh* was discovered and translated by British Assyrologist George Smith in the late nineteenth century. The

Epic of Gilgamesh initially caught the attention of Biblical critics for its episode of the "Mesopotamian Noah," that is, the character Utnapishtim, who, like his later Biblical counterpart, was advised by the gods to build a great boat to avoid an imminent, disastrous flood. Equally fascinating for the window this epic opens to the ancient and far-removed Sumerian and Babylonian cultures, Gilgamesh's conflict with the gods, struggles against the forces of nature, and recognition of his own mortality mirrors the always contemporary endeavor to find one's place both in society and in the cosmos.

At the same time the *Epic of Gilgamesh* addresses these important metaphysical themes, it is also a story of two friends, Gilgamesh and Enkidu, and their devotion to one another even after death. All in all, the *Epic of Gilgamesh* contains everything readers have come to expect from great epic literature: fantastic geographies, exotic characters, exhausting quests, difficult journeys, heroic battles, and supernatural beings. It is, above all, the gripping story of an epic hero who is driven to meet his destiny and who rises to every challenge with high courage and fierce determination.

Author Biography

The *Epic of Gilgamesh* is not the product of a single author in the modern sense but was the progressive creation of several ancient Near Eastern cultures, specifically the cultures of Mesopotamia, the land between the Tigris and Euphrates Rivers. Originally an oral composition recited by communal storytellers, perhaps priests, to a listening audience, portions of the *Epic of Gilgamesh* were likely recited for many generations before being recorded by scribes in an archaic form of writing called cuneiform. Scribes wrote the ancient oral stories onto clay tablets with a sharply pointed, triangular stick, and the tablets telling the Gilgamesh story were kept in royal libraries. The most famous royal library was that of Ashurbanipal, king of Babylon during the seventh century BCE, but portions of the *Epic of Gilgamesh*, from very different time periods, have also been found. The individual stories of the Gilgamesh cycle were first written in cuneiform by ancient Sumerian scribes about four thousand years ago. The story passed from the Sumerians through succeeding civilizations to the Babylonians, who added to or otherwise adapted the Gilgamesh stories to their own culture until a so-called Standard Version of the *Epic of Gilgamesh* coalesced about 1500 BCE.

The *Epic of Gilgamesh* was then lost for thousands of years beneath the sand and rubble of the ancient Near East until archaeologists began to excavate and discover the ancient tablets during the nineteenth century. English translation of the *Epic of Gilgamesh*, which began in the 1880s with George Smith, is the product of many scholars' work and many years of archaeological investigation, historical inquiry, and linguistic research. Even with all of this academic reconstruction, Assyrologists cannot be completely sure of all the details of the *Epic of Gilgamesh*. Some portions of the story are missing, lost in the broken off sections of cuneiform tablets. Aspects of the ancient languages involved are so obscure and foreign that scholars cannot be sure of an exact translation. At many points, the extant work is at best a reconstruction of what the story said originally, but as new tablets are discovered, knowledge of the *Epic of Gilgamesh* increases.

Originally, the *Epic of Gilgamesh* was written as poetry, but not in the kind of rhyming verse that typifies English verse. The style was closer to the alliterative tradition of a poem such as *Beowulf.* One available and easily read translation of the *Epic of Gilgamesh* is the 1972 Penguin Classic paperback version by N. K. Sandars, but many other editions are also available. Sandars' translation has turned the poetic form of the so-called Standard, or Babylonian, Version of the *Epic of Gilgamesh* into a narrative form. Moreover, the *Epic of Gilgamesh* probably appeared originally as five or six separate Sumerian stories that were adapted by later cultures, especially the Babylonians. The current translation has divided the original story found in twelve tablets into eight sections: seven chapters and a prologue. Therefore, the *Epic of Gilgamesh* has been transformed once again in language, style, and structure for contemporary readers.

Plot Summary

Prologue

The Prologue to the *Epic of Gilgamesh* establishes Gilgamesh's stature as the special creation of the gods: He is two-thirds divine and one-third human. The strongest and wisest of all humans, he is also the renowned builder and king of the great city of Uruk. The Prologue sets the story in the distant past, in "the days before the flood," when Gilgamesh himself etched the whole story in stone.

1. The Coming of Enkidu

Gilgamesh, king of Uruk, is the strongest of all men, but he is not a kind ruler. He takes advantage of his people. So the people of Uruk describe his abuses to Anu, god of Uruk, who asks Aruru, goddess of creation, to create an equal, "his second self" to oppose Gilgamesh and leave them at peace. Aruru creates Enkidu out of the raw stuff of nature. Enkidu is a fearfully strong, uncultured "wild man" with long hair and coarse features who runs with the beasts and eats grass. A trapper sees Enkidu at a watering hole for three straight days, and the trapper, amazed and dumbfounded, tells his father about the wild man who disrupts his snares. The father advises the son to find Gilgamesh, who gives him a "harlot" or temple courtesan to tame the wild man. The woman embraces Enkidu, cleans and clothes him, and teaches him civilized behavior. As a result, Enkidu becomes a man. When Enkidu is brought to Uruk, Gilgamesh aborts his impending marriage to Ishtar, the goddess of love and war, and meets Enkidu, who has challenged him, in the street. They fight, and after Gilgamesh throws Enkidu, they embrace and become friends.

Media Adaptations

- Czech musician Bohuslav Martinu composed the choral piece *Epic of Gilgamesh*, which was first performed in 1955. Martinu's work is often performed and widely available in recorder formats. A 2009 reissue of a 1989 performance of his *Epic of Gilgamesh*, conducted by Zdenek Kosler and performed by the Slovak Philharmonic Orchestra, is available on compact disc from

Marco-Polo.

- The opera *Gilgamesh* was written by Serbian director and librettist Arsenije Milosevic and composed by Croatian-Italian musician Rudolf Brucci. It premiered November 2, 1986, at the Serbian National Theatre in Novi Sad.

- Shotaro Ishinomori penned the story that inspired the anime series *Gilgamesh*, directed by Masahiko Murata. Set in the present, rather than the past, the series is influenced by the original epic. It first aired on television in 2003 and 2004 and is available on DVD from ADV Films.

- An e-book of the Old Babylonian version of the *Epic of Gilgamesh* is available online from the Project Gutenberg.

- An unabridged audio book adaptation of Stephen Mitchell's *Gilgamesh: A New English Version* is available on compact disc or download from Recorded Books. Produced in 2004, it is narrated by George Guidall.

- Adapa Films created a dramatization titled *Epic of Gilgamesh: Tablet XI*. Following the events of the eleventh tablet, Utnapishtim regales

Gilgamesh with the story of the flood that he alone survived. Filmed in Akkadian with English subtitles, this movie is available online on DVD from the Adapa Films. NO production date was available at the online source, http://offlinenetworks.com/adapa.

2. The Forest Journey

Enlil, father of the gods, establishes Gilgamesh's destiny to be king and achieve great feats, but Enkidu is "oppressed by [the] idleness" of living in Uruk. In order to establish his eternal reputation, to "leave behind me a name that endures," Gilgamesh proposes to travel with Enkidu to the Land of the Cedars and kill its guardian, the fearsome giant Humbaba. Gilgamesh prepares for the journey both by making a sacrifice to Shamash, who gives him the natural elements as allies; by forging a set of formidable weapons, including an axe, bow, and shield; and by seeking the intervention of his mother Ninsun, who adopts Enkidu as her own. Now brothers as well as companions, Gilgamesh and Enkidu begin their journey. On the way, Gilgamesh has three dreams, which though frightening portend a successful end to his quest. Humbaba, the guardian of the cedars, can hear an animal stir from many miles away, and he has seven fearsome "splendors" as weapons. After they arrive at the grove, Gilgamesh and Enkidu send Humbaba into a rage by cutting down one of the sacred trees. After a fierce battle, Gilgamesh defeats Humbaba, who begs for his life. Gilgamesh nearly relents, saving Humbaba momentarily, but acting on Enkidu's strong warning, Gilgamesh cuts off the giant's head. They present Humbaba's head to Enlil, who rages at them for their actions and disburses Humbaba's seven auras across creation.

3. Ishtar and Gilgamesh, and the Death of Enkidu

After Gilgamesh slays Humbaba, Ishtar calls Gilgamesh back to be her groom by promising him many expensive gifts. Gilgamesh now flatly refuses her offer because of her "abominable behaviour," for he knows how badly Ishtar has treated her previous lovers, turning many of them from men into animals. Ishtar bristles at Gilgamesh's charges and urges her parents Anu and Antum to set loose the Bull of Heaven upon the city of Uruk and its ruler, Gilgamesh. Ishtar unleashes the great bull against Gilgamesh, but Gilgamesh and Enkidu together slay the bull, proving again their great prowess. Afterward, Enkidu has a dream in which a council of the gods has decreed that Enkidu must die for their deeds. Enkidu falls ill and curses the trapper and courtesan who brought him to Uruk, but Shamash reminds him how much good came from the trapper's and harlot's action. Enkidu has a second dream about the underworld and its inhabitants, which Gilgamesh interprets as an omen of death. Enkidu languishes ill for days before he dies, and Gilgamesh, who mourns for seven days, offers a moving lament and builds a noble statue in tribute to his friend.

4. The Search for Everlasting Life

In his despair, Gilgamesh begins a lengthy quest to find the answer to life's mysteries, especially the mystery of eternal life. He decides to seek out Utnapishtim "the Faraway," his ancient ancestor who "has entered the assembly of the gods" and received everlasting life. Sick at heart for the death of Enkidu and realizing more acutely his own mortality, Gilgamesh pushes on through the great mountains of Mashu, gate to the afterlife where the sun sets, where he defeats a band of lions. He then encounters the frightful Scorpion-Demon and his mate who guard Mashu and persuades them to let him enter. Gilgamesh travels through twelve leagues of darkness (twenty four hours) until he enters the garden of the gods. There, in turn, he meets Shamash, the sun god, who discourages his quest; Siduri, goddess of wine and the vines, who encourages him to "dance and be merry, feast and rejoice" and finally Urshanabi, the ferryman of Utnapishtim, who at first tells him his quest is futile but then takes him across the sea of death to Utnapishtim. On the other side of the sea, Gilgamesh recounts to Utnapishtim his journey, Enkidu's death, and his quest for eternal life. In response to Gilgamesh's questioning about his search for eternal life, Utnapishtim replies flatly, "There is no permanence." Disheartened, Gilgamesh persists until Utnapishtim agrees to tell Gilgamesh "a mystery," the story of how he gained immortality.

5. The Story of the Flood

In the ancient city of Shurrupak on the Euphrates River, according to the Utnapishtim's tale, the clamor of humanity rises up to the gods and disturbs their peace. Enlil calls for the gods "to exterminate mankind." The council of the gods agrees, but Ea warns Utnapishtim secretly in a dream that a flood is coming. To protect her favorite, Ea tells Utnapishtim to build a boat and "take up into the boat the seed of all living creatures." It takes Utnapishtim seven days to build a boat of seven decks, and after loading it full of his family, wealth, kin, and craftsmen, he rides out a seven-day storm. On the seventh day, the boat runs aground and Utnapishtim releases three birds in succession: the dove and swallow return, but the raven does not, indicating the presence of dry land. After Utnapishtim makes a sacrifice, over which the gods "gathered like flies," Ishtar presents her opulent necklace as a remembrance of the disaster, and Enlil makes restitution for his rash act by giving Utnapishtim and his wife immortality.

6. The Return

Utnapishtim puts Gilgamesh's desire for eternal life

to the test: "only prevail against sleep for six days and seven nights." Gilgamesh, however, quickly falls asleep as the result of his exertions. To prove that Gilgamesh has slept, Utnapishtim has his wife bake a loaf of bread for each of the seven days Gilgamesh sleeps. After Utnapishtim wakes Gilgamesh, Gilgamesh sees the proof and despairs, realizing more clearly than ever that "death inhabits my room." Utnapishtim then curses Urshanabi for bringing Gilgamesh to him and commands Urshanabi to bathe and dress Gilgamesh, who is covered in grime and clothed in skins. Utnapishtim's wife asks Utnapishtim not to send Gilgamesh away empty handed. In response, Utnapishtim reveals the location to a secret underwater plant that will "restore his lost youth to a man." Gilgamesh harvests the plant and proposes to take it back to Uruk with him, but when Gilgamesh stops at an oasis to bathe, a serpent from the well steals and eats the plant, sloughs off its skin, and disappears again. Gilgamesh bewails the loss-his last chance for immortality-and returns to Uruk. At Uruk, Gilgamesh engraves his exploits in stone to testify to his greatness.

7. Death of Gilgamesh

Gilgamesh has fulfilled his destiny to be king, but his dream of eternal life eludes him. The narration concludes with a lament on Gilgamesh's mortality, a description of the funerary ritual, and a paean of praise to Gilgamesh; his family, his servants, the city of Uruk, and the pantheon of gods all mourn his loss.

Adad

Adad is a storm god who endows Gilgamesh with courage at his birth.

Antum

Antum is the wife of Anu, the sky god or god of the heavens, and mother of Ishtar. Ishtar complains to her parents Anu and Antum when Gilgamesh refuses her offer of marriage and describes how she has abused her previous lovers.

Anu

Anu is god of the firmament, the patron god of Uruk, husband of Antum, and father of Ishtar. The *Epic of Gilgamesh* opens with a description of "the temple of blessed Eanna for the god of the firmament Anu." Gilgamesh dreams of a falling meteor, which portends Enkidu's arrival and calls it "the stuff of Anu."

Anunnaki

The Anunnaki are gods of the underworld, also known as the seven judges of hell. Their sacred dwellings are in the Forest of Cedars, guarded by

Humbaba. They also appear in Utnapishtim's account of the great flood as forerunners of the storm.

Aruru

Aruru is the goddess of creation, or Mother Goddess, who fashions Enkidu from clay.

Aya

Aya is the goddess of the dawn and wife of the sun god Shamash.

Belit-Sheri

Belit-Sheri is the "recorder of the gods" and scribe of the underworld who "keeps the book of death." She appears in Enkidu's dream of the afterlife.

Dumuzi

See Tammuz

Ea

Ea, called "the wise," is god of the sweet waters and of the arts. He breaks rank with the council of the gods and warns Utnapishtim of the impending flood. Ea is the Akkadian version of the older, Sumerian god Enki.

Endukagga

Endukagga is a god who governs in the underworld, along with Nindukugga.

Enki

See Ea

Enkidu

Enkidu is Gilgamesh's "second self" and faithful companion. Aruru fashions Enkidu from clay in the image of Anu. Enkidu is a "wild," primitive, uncivilized man who has both the hardened physique and virtue of Ninurta, the god of war; the long hair of Ninursa, goddess of corn; and the hairy body of Samuqan, god of cattle.

Ennugi

Ennugi is the "watcher over canals" and god of irrigation.

Ereshkigal

Ereshkigal is the queen of the underworld, who appears in Enkidu's dream of the afterlife. She is the wife of Nergal. Ereshkigal was also known as Irkalla, another name for the underworld.

Gilgamesh

Gilgamesh is the protagonist or main character of the *Epic of Gilgamesh*. An historical figure who ruled Uruk around 2700 BCE, Gilgamesh is the child of Lugulbanda, a divine king, and Ninsun. Gilgamesh is the semi-divine king of Uruk; the special charge of Shamash, the sun god; sometime consort of Ishtar, goddess of love and war; and builder of the mighty city of Uruk and its great temple Eanna. Originally the subject of at least five Sumerian myths, Gilgamesh becomes the main character in a Babylonian revision of those earlier stories. In later myths he is a judge of the underworld and is sometimes called its king. The epic narrates the transformation of Gilgamesh from a selfish and thoughtless young ruler into a wise and well-loved king and reveals Gilgamesh's gradual understanding of his own mortality.

Hanish

Hanish is the herald of storms and bad weather.

He appears with Shullat at the beginning of the storm in Utnapishtim's story of the flood.

Harlot

The harlot is a temple courtesan in the cult of Ishtar at the great temple Eanna. The harlot is the woman Gilgamesh sends back with the trapper to pacify Enkidu. She initiates Enkidu into the ways of sex and culture, teaching him to eat, drink, and clothe himself. After her ministrations, Enkidu is unable to return to the wilderness. She then takes Enkidu to Uruk where he challenges Gilgamesh.

Humbaba

Humbaba is a fearsome monster appointed by Enlil to protect the Forest of Cedars. In a fierce battle, Gilgamesh and Enkidu ultimately kill Humbaba and cut down the sacred cedars.

Irkalla

See Ereshkigal

Ishtar

Ishtar is the goddess of love and war and daughter of Anu and Antum. She is the patroness of Uruk, Gilgamesh's home city. She is fickle and at times spiteful, as demonstrated in her treatment of her former lovers and her wrath at Uruk after Gilgamesh spurns her advances. She inhabits Eanna, Uruk's fabulous temple, or ziggurat.

Ishullana

Ishullana is Anu's gardener, whom Ishtar loved and then turned into a blind mole after he rejected her.

Ki

See Ninhursag

Lugulbanda

Lugulbanda is one of the ancient kings of Uruk and Gilgamesh's guardian god and progenitor.

Lugulbanda is the subject of his own epic cycle.

Mammetum

Mammetum is the "mother of destinies." Utnapishtim reveals that Mammetum, with the Anunnaki, "together ... decree the fates of men. Life and death they allot but the day of death they do not disclose."

Man-Scorpion

Described as "half man and half dragon," the Man-Scorpion and his mate are guardians of Mashu, the mountains of the rising and setting sun. They let Gilgamesh pass through to the garden of the gods.

Namtar

Namtar, the god of death, is the servant of Ereshkigal, queen of the underworld.

Nergal

Nergal is an underworld god and husband of Ereshkigal. During Utnapishtim's flood, "Nergal pulled out the dams of the nether waters."

Neti

Neti is gatekeeper of the underworld and servant of Ereshkigal.

Nindukugga

Nindukugga is a god who governs the underworld with Endukagga.

Ningal

Ningal is mother of the sun god, Shamash, and wife of the moon god Sin.

Ningizzida

Ningizzida is the god of the serpent and lord of the tree of life.

Ningursu

See Ninurta

Ninhursag

Ninhursag is the goddess of growth and vegetation, and mother of Enlil. She is known by many other names, including Ki, Ninki, and Ninmah.

Ninki

See Ninhursag

Ninlil

Ninlil is the wife of Enlil and goddess of heaven, earth, and air or spirit.

Ninsun

The goddess Ninsun, called "the well-beloved and wise," is mother of Gilgamesh and wife of Lugulbanda. Prior to Gilgamesh and Enkidu's trip to kill Humbaba, Ninsun adopts Enkidu as her own, gives him a sacred necklace, and entrusts Gilgamesh's safety to him.

Ninurta

Ninurta is a warrior god and god of wells and canals. In the story of Utnapishtim, Ninurta is one of those who caused the flood with Nergal. He is also known as Ningursu.

Nisaba

Nisaba is the goddess of corn. She gives Enkidu his long, flowing hair.

Puzur-Amurri

Puzur-Amurri is the steersman and navigator of Utnapishtim's great boat during the flood.

Samuqan

Samuqan is the god of cattle and of herds. He gives Enkidu his rough, hair-covered hide.

Scorpion-Demon

See Man-Scorpion

Shamash

One of the chief gods, Shamash is the sun god, lawgiver, and judge who is evoked in blessing and protection throughout the *Epic of Gilgamesh*.

Shullat

Shullat is a minor god under Shamash who works with Hanish to herald bad weather, as happened at the beginning of the great flood.

Shulpae

Shulpae is god of the feast. Sacrifices are made to Shulpae at funerals.

Siduri

Siduri is goddess of the vine, who at first bars Gilgamesh from passage through the garden of the gods, but then tells him, "When the gods created man they allotted to him death, but they retained life in their own keeping."

Sillah

Sillah is the mother of one of Ishtar's lovers.

Sin

Sin is the moon god, to whom Gilgamesh prays as he travels through dark mountain passes populated by lions on his way to Mashu.

Tammuz

Tammuz is the god of shepherds, sheepfolds, and vegetation. He is one of Ishtar's consorts. In older, Sumerian times, he was known as Dumuzi.

Trapper

The trapper is the first person to encounter Enkidu, who had sabotaged his traps. Enkidu later curses the trapper for introducing him to civilization and its difficulties.

Ubara-Tutu

Ubara-Tutu is the ancient king of Shurrupak and Utnapishtim's father.

Urshanabi

Urshanabi is the boatman who takes Gilgamesh over the waters of death to Utnapishtim. Utnapishtim curses Urshanabi for bringing a mortal to him across the sea of death. After he helps Gilgamesh back to health and vigor, Urshanabi returns with Gilgamesh to Uruk.

Utnapishtim

Favored by the god Ea, Utnapishtim is warned of Enlil's plan to destroy humanity through a flood. Utnapishtim, at Ea's command, builds a huge square boat, seven decks high and one-hundred twenty cubits per side, in seven days. He seals it with pitch, stores away supplies, and rides out the seven-day storm in it.

Vampire-Demon

The vampire-demon is a supernatural being who appears in Enkidu's dream of the underworld. In the dream, he attacks and smothers Enkidu.

Heroism

Heroes are courageous and often act selflessly or for the greater good; however, mythologist Joseph Campbell defines a hero not by valor but by the steps of a hero's journey. This journey is described in Campbell's book *The Hero With a Thousand Faces*. The *Epic of Gilgamesh* is a hero's journey, beginning with Gilgamesh's reluctance to act, as seen in his boredom, his abuse of his people, and the need for the divine to intercede. Enkidu not only aids Gilgamesh throughout his journey but also functionally completes him as a person. Despite Gilgamesh's growth as a hero by Campbell's definition, he is still selfish throughout, as shown in the adventure to the Forest of the Cedars, a sacred place that Gilgamesh nonetheless pillages for wood and self-aggrandizement. Enkidu's death deeply affects Gilgamesh. Wracked with grief, Gilgamesh travels to the underworld in search of immortality for himself. He fails to achieve his goal but is told repeatedly by characters such as the goddess Siduri and by Utnapishtim that mortality has its own virtues, which he should appreciate. Whether Gilgamesh is able to enjoy the remainder of his mortal days is not recorded in this epic, but the completion of his journey, by Campbell's definition, occurs when he returns to Uruk and has his adventures carved upon a stone, therefore bringing this appreciation of the human experience back to the people.

Topics for Further Study

- Compare and contrast an episode in N. K. Sandars' narrative version of the *Epic of Gilgamesh* with David Ferry's poetic version or one of the versions that follow the original twelve-tablet structure of the story. How do the versions differ in their use of language and their organization on the page? Do they differ in their symbolic or thematic emphases? Write a comparative essay explaining the similarities and differences.

- Locate the five independent myths of the Sumerian song-cycle featuring Gilgamesh ("Gilgamesh and Agga of Kish" "Gilgamesh and the Land of the Living" "Gilgamesh and the Bull of Heaven" "Gilgamesh, Enkidu, and the Netherworld" and "The Death of Gilgamesh") in James Pritchard's, *Ancient Near Eastern Texts Relating to the Old Testament*. Choose one, read it carefully, and see if you can identify which portion(s) or details of the Sumerian myth have been incorporated into the Babylonian Standard Version and which have been excluded. Compose an electronic presentation to share with your class that details the transformation of this story.

- Many contemporary movies feature a hero and a counterpart or buddy. Often these two characters are as different as Gilgamesh and Enkidu, but together they make a complete team. Select a current "buddy movie" and, using the *Epic of Gilgamesh* as a guide, analyze the epic qualities of that movie. Consider how the buddies are alike or different, how they react to the opposite sex, what quest they set out to achieve, and what great enemy or evil they face. With a partner, prepare a dramatic presentation that gives your findings from this examination.

- Drawing on other subjects of study such as biology, geography, art, archaeology, and history, create a collage showing the elements of ancient Mesopotamian life depicted in the *Epic of Gilgamesh* or a diorama (picture box) of an ancient ziggurat or temple. Reconstruct the architecture of the time; the different people who inhabited the cities; the jobs they performed; the crops they grew; the crafts they made; and clothing they wore.

- Research the hero's journey as described by mythologist Joseph Campbell in his book *The Hero with a Thousand Faces*. Campbell's hero's journey was a strong influence on the 1977 film *Star Wars Episode IV: A New Hope* but has its roots in myths about heroes such as the *Epic of Gilgamesh*. How many elements of the hero's journey are present in the film? How many elements are present in the epic? Which do you think is a better story and why, based on the hero's journey? Give a five-minute presentation to your class, with examples and visual aids.

Culture and Nature

The internal balance between physical and spiritual journeys in the *Epic of Gilgamesh* is matched by the contrast in the two main characters, Gilgamesh and Enkidu. As the epic opens, Gilgamesh embodies both the arrogance and the cultivation of high Sumerian culture. He is the king and epitomizes power, he is physically gifted and beautiful, but he is also haughty and abusive: He deflowers the maidens of his kingdom for his own pleasure and he presses the young men into his service.

By contrast, when he enters the story, Enkidu personifies the coarse physicality and vitality of the natural world: He is immensely strong, he lives and runs with the wild beasts, and he destroys the traps set by hunters. At a crucial early juncture in the epic, Gilgamesh, having heard about this "wild man," sends a courtesan to Enkidu. She transforms Enkidu's wildness through her sexual charms, and she teaches him table manners and correct behavior. Afterwards, the wild animals run away from Enkidu. The courtesan thereby brings Enkidu into the civilized world. Together, Gilgamesh, the cultivated ruler, and Enkidu, the civilized wild man, bond as complementary friends, and they begin a series of exploits to conquer Humbaba, that other forest creature, and the Bull of Heaven, the embodiment of natural disaster.

Identity and Relationship

As the semi-divine creation of Shamash, the sun

god, who gives him physical beauty, and Adad, the storm god, who gives him great courage, Gilgamesh is at the top of the social hierarchy. As king of Uruk, Gilgamesh has access to all the riches and pleasures his society can provide. In his lofty station, Gilgamesh has no need or desire for a relationship with others, for he seems to be complete in himself. However, Gilgamesh is also unsettled and "a man of many moods," an arrogant ruler who mistreats his people. He is, in other words, incomplete, lacking an ingredient essential to being fully human. The people of Uruk complain to Anu, god of Uruk, to intervene on their behalf, and Aruru, the goddess of creation, responds by creating Enkidu. Enkidu requires the moderating influences of civilization to become fully human. Incomplete when separated, but together and fulfilled in close relationship, Gilgamesh and Enkidu establish their true identities. Their identities are fulfilled through their relationship. Enkidu perishes before the end of the tale, and Gilgamesh is haunted by the death of his friend. This death is the catalyst for Gilgamesh's search for immortality. Thus, Gilgamesh carries the legacy of his friend back to Uruk, where he dies a well-loved king.

Humanity and Divinity

Human interaction with the gods, and the gods' intervention in human events, is a standard hallmark of epic literature, and the *Epic of Gilgamesh* is no exception. From beginning to end of the tale, the supernatural world intersects the physical plane.

Persons, places, and all manner of things are closely associated with patron deities. The interplay of humanity and divinity is closely allied to the question of identity and relationship throughout the epic. Characters take on the attributes of deities associated with them. Gilgamesh is a mixture of both human and divine, but emphasizing the divine. Enkidu incarnates precisely the opposite proportions, favoring the human. At the same time that the epic invokes the gods throughout the narrative, they seem distant from the action, interfering only when pressed or perturbed. The gods are also clearly anthropomorphic, quite human in their petty jealousy, bickering, and irritation with irascible humans.

Mortality and Immortality

During the course of the epic, Gilgamesh, as king of Uruk, progresses from the highest social station to the lowest example of a human being-pale, starved, and clothed in skins during his encounter with Utnapishtim. The crux of this journey is the death of Gilgamesh's beloved comrade, Enkidu. During the first half of the tale, Gilgamesh and Enkidu bring death to all enemies in their quest to establish their eternal reputations; during the second half, Gilgamesh lives with the haunting memory of Enkidu's death. As Gilgamesh tells Utnapishtim: "Because of my brother I am afraid of death; because of my brother I stray through the wilderness. His fate lies heavy upon me. How can I be silent, how can I rest? He is dust and I shall die also and be laid in the earth forever." Having turned to great exploits, huge building projects, and epic journeys to secure his fame, Gilgamesh must die, but his memory lives on in the story of his life. The gods do not give Gilgamesh immortality, but the legends of his life are preserved on the stone tablets of his epic adventure.

Epic Literature

In *A Glossary of Literary Terms*, literary scholar M. H. Abrams lists five essential characteristics of epic literature: (1) a hero of national and/or cosmic importance; (2) an expansive setting, perhaps even worldwide; (3) superhuman deeds; (4) supernatural forces and deities take part in events; and (5) the language of a ceremonial performance, much elevated over ordinary speech. The *Epic of Gilgamesh* has each of these characteristics.

First, Gilgamesh, as ruler of Uruk and son of a goddess, is a figure of national importance. It is interesting that he is, nonetheless, incomplete without his friend Enkidu, who seems to be of no cosmic or national significance except as Gilgamesh's friend. Their relationship may have had meaning to the Sumerian, Assyrian, and Babylonian audiences that modern readers cannot grasp.

Second, the scope of this story begins and ends at the great city of Uruk in Mesopotamia, the land between two rivers and traditionally known as the cradle of civilization. Uruk was the first city built by humankind. Gilgamesh and Enkidu also travel to the Forest of the Cedars, a holy place, and later Gilgamesh journeys to the land of the dead. The setting of this epic is grand, sweeping, and aweinspiring to listeners.

Third, Gilgamesh and Enkidu, his adopted brother, are the strongest of men. When they fight, walls shake. Only they are capable of taking on the terrible monster Humbaba, who guards the Forest of the Cedars, but their success requires both wits and strength. They also kill the Bull of Heaven to prevent drought, and Gilgamesh conquers many wild animals in the lands at the end of the world, where he begins his journey to the underworld realm. Through these feats, Gilgamesh is shown to be the most powerful man.

Fourth, the gods are involved throughout this tale. Gilgamesh's mother is the goddess Ninlil, whom he goes to for dream interpretations and to ask her to name his friend Enkidu as her son so that they may be brothers. Enkidu is fashioned from clay by the goddess Aruru to be Gilgamesh's match and distract him from tormenting the people of Uruk. Gilgamesh's patron deity is the sun god Shamash, whom he appeals to for help. Enlil, a major deity in the Babylonian pantheon, intervenes after Gilgamesh and Enkidu kill Humbaba, dispersing Humbaba's auras to the rest of creation.

Fifth, the *Epic of Gilgamesh* is structured in a formal way that betrays its origins as a oral performance piece. The elevated, formal language and repeated formulaic phrases are characteristic of epic literature. In fact, the dialogue sounds stilted and rehearsed, as if read for a formal occasion. During chapter 2, "The Forest Journey," Gilgamesh calls out for assistance: "By the life of my mother Ninsun who gave me birth, and by the life of my father, divine Lugulbanda, let me live to be the wonder of my mother, as when she nursed me on her lap." These formal invocations of deity give the task an elevated stature and a sense of being a holy mission that Gilgamesh undertakes for his city and his divine heritage. In a later example, as he faces Humbaba in battle, Gilgamesh beseeches his patron god: "O glorious Shamash, I have followed the road you commanded but now if you send no succor how shall I escape?" The use of "apostrophe," a figure of speech denoted by "O," indicates a formal invocation of a person or personification who is not present.

Another important element of the elevated style of the *Epic of Gilgamesh* is its inclusion of "laments," the formal poems of praise and songs of grief that the living give on behalf of the dead. The finest example in the poem is Gilgamesh's lament for Enkidu, which begins:

> Hear me, great ones of Uruk, I weep for Enkidu, my friend. Bitterly moaning like a woman mourning I weep for my brother. You were the axe at my side, My hand's strength, the sword in my belt, the shield before me, A glorious robe, my fairest ornament, an evil Fate has robbed me.

Gilgamesh's heart-felt lament concludes with the mournful lines, "What is this sleep which holds you now?/You are lost in the dark and cannot hear me." Nearly all of these formal speeches also serve to summarize or rehearse the characters' attitudes or even the action in the story up to that point in the narrative.

Orality and Performance

One of the key attributes of the *Epic of Gilgamesh* is the sense of breathless immediacy of the story. The epic achieves this effect by placing the story in a setting that simulates the oral performance in which the story was originally performed. The opening lines provide a sense that this is not an ancient story, but one just occurring. The narrative first-person speaker of the Prologue places the reader at Uruk's city walls and erases the distance between that ancient time and the present time of telling the story, inviting the hearer (and reader) to feel present to the action. These walls, the narrative voice proclaims, are those of the great Gilgamesh and now I will tell you his story. This sense of immediacy continues throughout the epic.

In medias res

Traditionally, epics begin *in medias res* or "in the middle of things." Although this characteristic was originally applied to Greek and Roman epics such as the *Odyssey* and the *Iliad*, it is equally true of the *Epic of Gilgamesh*. The story begins not at the beginning of Gilgamesh's life, but somewhere in the middle. He is initially portrayed as a young, hot-headed king, heedless of the effect of actions and desires on the wellbeing of his people. One of the effects of this technique is to allow the reader to gauge the extent of Gilgamesh's development as a character.

Epithet

Another feature of the epic style is the use of epithets, usually adjectives or adjective phrases that reveal the attributes or personality of people, places, and things in the story: "strong-walled Uruk," "Humbaba whose name is 'Hugeness,'" "Shamash the Protector," and Utnapishtim "the Faraway." Epic epithets provide tags the assist the memory of the listener or reader. They also assist in recitation during a performance, serving as tags designed to move the speaker along easily.

Repetition

A characteristic of the epic that is closely related to its often formal, even stilted language, is its strategic use of repetition at various levels. There is hardly a moment, event, or speech that does not have a counterpart somewhere else in the tale.

Commonly called parallelism and antitheses, these contrasting and equivalent elements highlight comparison and/or contrast between paired elements. The repetitious elements can be examined in terms of structure, events, speeches, and numbers.

First, the epic has two parts, balanced structurally. The pivot of the story is Enkidu's death.

In the first half, Gilgamesh travels out into the Forest of the Cedars to slay Humbaba; in the second half he journeys into the realm of the gods to find Utnapishtim. Gilgamesh's early successes and personal glory contrast with his subsequent frustrations and hardships. Enkidu's physical presence if the first half contrasts with his palpable absence in the second half.

Repetition of events is seen in the first section: Gilgamesh and Enkidu are mirror images of one another; they slay two semi-divine monsters, Humbaba and the Bull of Heaven; and Gilgamesh has a series of dreams, matched by Enkidu's dreams later in the section. Events in the second half of the epic are often repetitions of earlier affairs, as when Gilgamesh's twelve-league journey through the Mashu's darkness pales in comparison to his one-hundred and twenty pole voyage across the waters of death. Finally, events in the second half mirror those in the first: Enkidu's funeral and Gilgamesh's lament for his dead friend are matched by Gilgamesh's funeral and Uruk's praise for its dead king, and Gilgamesh's voyage to find Utnapishtim parallels the earlier journey to the Cedar Forest.

Parts of a speech may be repeated from one character to the next or more tellingly, the entire speech may be repeated several times throughout a portion of the epic. The most significant instance of this technique occurs in chapter 4, "The Search for Everlasting Life." In his journey from the Country of the Living to the abode of the gods, Gilgamesh encounters Siduri, goddess of the vine and of wine;

Urshanabi, "the ferryman of Utnapishtim" who takes him across the waters of death; and finally Utnapishtim himself, the immortal human. Each encounter has the same structure.

Repetition of numbers come in patterns of two (two halves to the story or two carefully balanced main characters) or three (Gilgamesh's series of three dreams or the three quests of the tale) are well-known characteristics of epics. Seven is a symbolic number, sometimes in combination with two and three. Generally considered to be a perfect number or number of completion or wholeness, seven appears throughout the tale: the "seven sages" laid the foundations of Uruk; Enlil gives Humbaba "sevenfold terrors," or auras, with which to guard the forest; the gate of Uruk has seven bolts; and during the climactic battle with Humbaba, the giant unleashes the "seven splendors" against the pair of warriors; they fell "seven cedars" to provoke Humbaba's wrath, and they kill the giant with three blows to the neck, severing his head. This symbolic numerology continues especially in the story of the flood.

Development of the Epic

The *Epic of Gilgamesh* is the product of several civilizations of ancient Mesopotamia, those citystates of the Tigris-Euphrates river valley, in present-day Iraq. These cultures are, in turn, the Sumerians, the Akkadians or Babylonians, and the Assyrians. Scholars of the ancient Near East have determined that the *Epic of Gilgamesh* probably began as five separate Sumerian Gilgamesh stories (called "Gilgamesh and Agga of Kish;" "Gilgamesh and the Land of the Living;" "Gilgamesh and the Bull of Heaven;" "Gilgamesh, Enkidu, and the Netherworld;" and "The Death of Gilgamesh."). According to Jeffrey H. Tigay, who has written about the historical development of the epic in his *The Evolution of the Gilgamesh Epic*, estimates that the ancient oral tales about Gilgamesh probably were first written down, in cuneiform, about 2500 BCE by Sumerian scribes, although the earliest copies date from about 2100 BCE or about five hundred years after the historical Gilgamesh ruled Uruk.

These separate Sumerian tales were drawn together by a later Akkadian author (or authors) who adapted elements of the early stories into a more unified and complete epic. By this time the *Epic of Gilgamesh* had been widely circulated throughout the ancient Near East, with copies being found as far away as modern-day Palestine and Turkey. The *Epic of Gilgamesh* underwent other minor changes until it became formalized in a Standard Version, according to tradition, by the scribe Sinleqqiunninni around 1300 BCE. This is the most completely preserved version of the *Epic of Gilgamesh*, which archaeologists discovered in Ashurbanipal's library in Nineveh (685–27 BCE). This Standard Version is the basis for the translation by N. K. Sandars. However, the text will continue to evolve as archaeological discoveries are made and as scholars understand more fully the language, culture, and history of these ancient cultures and documents.

Events Historical and Mythological

The *Epic of Gilgamesh* is marked by both by the threat and the promise of its historical and physical setting. According to the famous Sumerian king list, Gilgamesh was an historical figure who reigned around 2700 BCE. He is called "the divine Gilgamesh ... [who] ruled 126 years," according to the "Sumerian King-List," translated by A. Leo Oppenheimer and published in *Ancient Near Eastern Texts Relating to the Old Testament*. Although it is impossible to know exactly, events like Gilgamesh's journey to the Forest of Cedars to defeat Humbaba may reflect the historical Uruk's trade relations, need for natural resources, and later struggles with neighboring citystates over vital resources such as wood.

Other details of daily life emerge from the story of Enkidu's gradual humanization at the hands of the temple harlot: "This transformation is achieved by eating bread, drinking beer, anointing oneself, and clothing oneself.... Bread, beer, oil, and clothing are the staples which were distributed as daily rations by the central institutions, such as the temple or palace, to a large segment of the population; these rations were their only means of subsistence," writes Johannes Renger in his essay "Mesopotamian Epic Literature," published in *Heroic Epic and Saga*. Furthermore, the cultures of the Tigris-Euphrates river valley depended upon the rivers for the rich soil that sustained local agriculture; at the same time the rivers brought life, frequent floods also wrecked havoc upon their cities and people. The *Epic of Gilgamesh* reveals these horrors, for Gilgamesh himself remarks that he looked over the wall and saw bodies floating in the river. Even the gods are affected, for Ishtar cries out like a woman in labor when she sees her people floating in the ocean "like the spawn of fish" during Utnapishtim's flood. Likewise, Ishtar's Bull of Heaven represents another of the ancient world's great fears: drought, famine, and natural disaster. Anu reminds Ishtar, "If I do what you desire there will be seven years of drought throughout Uruk when corn will be seedless husks." Thus, the ancient Mesopotamians were caught between the bounty of their river valley and the misery caused by its floods and droughts.

Finally, the *Epic of Gilgamesh* does not encompass all the stories recorded about Gilgamesh.

Gilgamesh himself is placed in the pantheons of gods as "an underworld deity, a judge there and sometimes called its king. His statues or figurines appear in burial rites for the dead, and his cult [official worship] was especially important in the month of Ab (July-August), when nature itself, as it were, expired," writes William L. Moran in the introduction to David Ferry's *Gilgamesh: A New Rendering in English Verse*.

Compare & Contrast

- **2000 BCE:** People of ancient Mesopotamia invent a writing system (cuneiform), use the wheel for transportation, and are skilled metalworkers. They produce crops in irrigated fields. They construct monumental buildings whose remains are visible after four thousand or more years.

  Today: Modern society, sometimes referred to as the Information Age, is characterized by rapid technological change, creating a global village, in which travel to or communication with any part of the world (or even beyond Earth) is possible within hours or even minutes. Increased human intervention in natural processes solves problems and creates them.

Agribusiness greatly increases food production and wreaks havoc with ecosystems. Genetic engineering creates new organisms, and extinction rates soar among various species because of global climate change.

- **2000 BCE:** The society of ancient Mesopotamia, is highly stratified and dominated mostly by men. The priestly caste and ruling elite control power and wealth. Power is concentrated in individual citystates rather than larger administrative units and wielded by a divinely instituted monarchy. Status is determined by birth, with little chance for advancement or education. Warfare is limited in scope and localized in space.

Today: Developed countries in the West have international power and wealth and consume most of the world's resources. Populations in developing countries in the East and in Africa struggle with extreme poverty and lower life expectancy. Most power is wielded by men, and church and state are separate in many western countries.

- **2000 BCE:** The economy of ancient Mesopotamia is agrarian, based on domesticated livestock and on the yearly cycles of flood and soil replenishment. Food supply is highly susceptible to ecological disruptions, such as drought or salinization of the soil.

Industry includes traditional crafts, textiles, and large-scale building projects of lumber and baked brick. During this time, the first large-scale urban centers develop, such as Uruk, with populations near 50,000.

Today: Modern economy is industrial and commercial. Even agriculture is big business. Risk of famine is curbed by chemical and genetic interventions, although longterm health concerns are voiced. The biggest metropolitan areas, such as Shanghai, New York City, and Mexico City exceed 20 million people.

The World's First City

Uruk, the world's first city, grew out of two small, agricultural settlements founded during the fifth millennium BCE that merged during the fourth millennium BCE and was able to exert military and political influence on the surrounding countryside and its settlements. This urbanization was a catalyst for stratified society and the comparable growth of other settlements into urban centers. The world's first cities were characterized by centralized distribution of goods; specialized production; large-scale architecture, such as the protective wall around Uruk, which required labor organization to achieve; and social stratification, which by the time of Gilgamesh's rule circa 2700 BCE was firmly inherited rather than achieved. Occupation of Uruk peaked around 2900 BCE, then fell off until it was abandoned in the mid-seventh century CE. The prevailing theory surrounding Uruk's decline is that the Euphrates River shifted its course from northeast to southwest of the city, perhaps flooding it for a period of time.

History and Recovery of the Epic of Gilgamesh

The critical reception of the *Epic of Gilgamesh* parallels the history of ancient Near Eastern archaeology between 1850 and the early 2000s. The *Epic of Gilgamesh* first came to light in tablets from the palace library of Ashurbanipal, king of Assyria (685–27 BCE), in Nineveh. The *Epic of Gilgamesh* is comprised of twelve fragmented clay tablets inscribed in cuneiform. Since that initial discovery, portions of the tale have surfaced throughout the region, from different time periods and in several different languages. By comparing the differences among the tablets and between various versions of the story, scholars have been able to reconstruct the history of the epic's composition. This history is complex and may not ever be fully known; however, it seems Mohave four main phases: the period of oral composition and circulation; the Sumerian tales of Gilgamesh; the Akkadian and Babylonian epics; and the Standard Version.

First, the historical Gilgamesh ruled Uruk, in southern Mesopotamia, around 2700 BCE, and a variety of historical artifacts confirm his existence. As is the custom of traditional cultures, stories of the king's exploits circulated among the populace and were repeated orally before being written down, probably about 2500 BCE.

Second, the Sumerians inscribed into clay tablets at least five separate Gilgamesh stories, the earliest of which among those known tablets dates from around 2100 BCE. These stories are known as "Gilgamesh and Agga of Kish" "Gilgamesh and the Land of the Living" "Gilgamesh and the Bull of Heaven" "Gilgamesh, Enkidu, and the Netherworld" and "The Death of Gilgamesh." It is important to note that these stories have little in common with each other except for having the same main character. They were not joined as a whole, nor did they share an overriding theme.

Third, these separate Sumerian stories became the raw material for the Babylonian (or Akkadian) *Epic of Gilgamesh*, composed about 1700 BCE. The Babylonian transcribers combined aspects of the earlier Sumerian stories to create the unified story of Gilgamesh's search for the meaning of life and his struggle against death. This Babylonian version also introduced several important changes, including transforming Enkidu from Gilgamesh's servant, as he is in the Sumerian tales, to an equal and companion; adding the hymn-like Prologue and conclusion and increasing the use of formulaic sayings and set-pieces; and incorporating the ancient legend of Utnapishtim and the great flood. The Babylonian version became known throughout the ancient Near East in a variety of languages.

Finally, the *Epic of Gilgamesh* became fixed in the so-called Standard Version, attributed to the author Sinleqqiunninni, who lived about 1300 BCE.

This Standard Version is the one that was found in Ashurbanipal's library.

Utnapishtim: The Mesopotamian Noah

Although at its discovery the *Epic of Gilgamesh* was immediately recognized for its literary and historical value, it gained widespread attention for its account of Utnapishtim and the flood. The story of the flood is found in Tablet XI of the *Epic of Gilgamesh* and is itself derived from an earlier story, "The Myth of Atrahasis." What most intrigued readers were the parallels between Utnapishtim and the Old Testament story of Noah and the Flood, found in Genesis 6:1–9:18. What shocked them even more is that the Utnapishtim episode predates, or is earlier than, the biblical account of Noah and the ark. Alexander Heidel, in *The Gilgamesh Epic and Old Testament Parallels*, explores the correlations between Noah's story and that of Utnapishtim. For example, Heidel points out that an assembly of gods directs Utnapishtim to build his boat, but only a single deity directs Noah to build his. Also according to the Old Testament, Noah is selected because he is righteous, unlike all other wicked people, by the judgmental god of monotheistic Judaism. Another difference is that the boat built by Utnapishtim is square with seven decks, which mirrors the design of the Mesopotamian ziggurat (step-temple). Whereas Noah's boat is more realistically boatshaped (long and narrow) and has three decks and a door. In the Utnapishtim version the storm lasts seven days; in the Noah story the storm lasts forty days.

New Interpretations

In 2004, Stephen Mitchell published *Gilgamesh: A New English Version* to critical favor and some controversy. Mitchell, an acclaimed translator specializing in epics, crafted a version of this ancient tale (using extant English translations) that brings it to life for the general reader. He compared the different accounts of the *Epic of Gilgamesh* to synthesize his own and used his imagination to fill in where clay tablets left the story incomplete. In a similar vein but with a different result, British poet Derrek Hines wrote a postmodern version of the epic in his book *Gilgamesh*, also published in 2004. Hines takes even more liberties with the narrative, introducing modern elements in an effort to make the ancient story feel as alive for twenty-first century readers as it once did for third millennium BCE listeners.

Sources

Abrams, M. H., *Glossary of Literary Terms*, 5th ed., Holt, Rinehart, and Winston, 1988, p. 52.

Campbell, Joseph, *The Hero with a Thousand Faces*, Princeton University Press, 1972.

Heidel, Alexander, *The Gilgamesh Epic and Old Testament Parallels*, 2nd ed., University of Chicago Press, 1949, pp. 224–69.

May, Herbert G., and Bruce M. Metzger, eds., *New Oxford Annotated Bible with the Apocrypha*, Oxford University Press, 1962.

Moore, Steven, "Carved in Stone," in *Washington Post*, November 14, 2004, p. T6.

Moran, William, "Introduction," in *Gilgamesh: A New Rendering in English Verse*, translated by David Ferry, Noonday Press, 1992, p. ix.

Olson, Ray, Review of *Gilgamesh*, in *Booklist*, Vol. 101, No. 4, October 15, 2004, p. 381.

Oppenheimer, A. Leo, trans., "Sumerian King-List," in *Ancient Near Eastern Texts Relating to the Old Testament*, edited by James A. Pritchard, Princeton University Press, 1950, p. 266.

Postgate, J. N., *Early Mesopotamia: Society and Economy at the Dawn of History*, Routledge, 1992, pp. 22–50.

Renger, Johannes M., "Mesopotamian Epic

Literature," in *Heroic Epic and Saga: An Introduction to the World's Great Folk Epics*, edited by Felix J. Oinas, Indiana University Press, 1978, p. 44.

Review of *Gilgamesh: A New English Version*, in *Publishers Weekly*, Vol. 251, No. 33, August 16, 2004, p. 41.

Sandars, N. K., *Epic of Gilgamesh: An English Version with an Introduction*, rev. ed., Penguin Books, 1972.

Tigay, Jeffrey H., *The Evolution of the Gilgamesh Epic*, University of Pennsylvania Press, 1982, pp. 248–50.

Further Reading

Dalley, Stephanie, trans., *Myths from Mesopotamia: Creation, the Flood, and Others*, Oxford World Classics, Oxford University Press, 2009.

> This excellent collection includes two versions of the *Epic of Gilgamesh* as well as the Mesopotamian creation epic (the *Enuma Elish*) and other myths associated with Gilgamesh and ancient Mesopotamian civilization. The literary material follows the cuneiform closely. Scholarly annotations are also included.

Damrosch, David, *The Buried Book: The Loss and Rediscovery of the Great "Epic of Gilgamesh,"* Henry Holt, 2007.

> Damrosch presents an engaging account of how the clay tablets of the Gilgamesh epic were unearthed and sent to England in the mid-nineteenth century, where they were deciphered by Assyrologist George Smith.

Ferry, David, *Gilgamesh: A New Rendering in English Verse*, Farrar, Straus and Giroux, 1993.

> Ferry's book is a lyrical, evocative transformation of the *Epic of*

Gilgamesh into verse couplets.

Ferry follows the twelve tablet format and includes brief notes at the end of his translation.

This book is a poetic achievement informed by sound scholarship.

Foster, Benjamin R., trans., *The Epic of Gilgamesh*, edited by Benjamin R. Foster, Norton Critical Edition, Norton, 2001.

> Foster, an Assyrologist at Yale University, provides new translations of the Gilgamesh epic and related Sumerian literature. New critical essays by respected scholars such as William Moran and Thorkild Jacobsen are also included.

Katz, Solomon H., and Fritz Maytag, "Brewing an Ancient Beer," in *Archaeology*, Vol. 44, No. 4, 1991, pp. 24–27.

> Katz's article is part of a debate over whether ancient Mesopotamians first began to gather and domesticate grain for the production of bread or for the production of beer.

Matthews, Roger, *The Archaeology of Mesopotamia: Theories and Approaches*, Routledge, 2003.

> With a fine prose style, Matthews presents this knowledgeable and highly readable study of archeology in ancient Mesopotamia.

Mitchell, Stephen, *Gilgamesh: A New English Version*, New Press, 2004.

> Acclaimed translator, Stephen Mitchell offers a fresh translation of the epic, which he sees as the world's first novel, concerned with the universal theme of growing up.

Pollock, Susan, *Ancient Mesopotamia*, Cambridge University Press, 1999.

> Pollock provides an archaeologist's perspective on the ancient Near East in her description of the homes, daily life, economy, architecture, landscape, and religion of the ancient people who lived between the two rivers.

Rothman, Mitchell S., ed., *Uruk Mesopotamia and Its Neighbors: Cross-cultural Interactions and Their Consequences in the Era of State Formation* (School of American Research Advanced Seminar), James Currey, 2002.

> This collection presents essays by leading experts on the Uruk period who discuss the rise of the Mesopotamian city-state.

Suggested Search Terms

Babylonian literature

Enkidu epic AND Mesopotamia

Gilgamesh Sumerian AND literature